What Am I Doing in Casablanca?

COLLECTION ONE

AMANDA WILSON

authorHOUSE®

AuthorHouse™
1663 Liberty Drive
Bloomington, IN 47403
www.authorhouse.com
Phone: 833-262-8899

Published by AuthorHouse 03/22/2021

ISBN: 978-1-6655-1577-1 (sc)
ISBN: 978-1-6655-1576-4 (e)

CONTENTS

INTRODUCTION

Welp, no turning back now! We're both here—and I'm about to do something I never thought I'd ever do. So, peek-a-boo!

Welcome to my art; also welcome to my psyche, my mind, my thoughts (and well, maybe also a little bit of socially acceptable emotional instability.) This collection would scare my younger self half-to-death! In fact, she's still in here—she's screaming at me to take pieces out, change the lines, and soften the blows for your reading pleasure.

I simply can't. I decided to publish these poems because I'm proud of them, and I'm proud of what they represent. They are, and will always be, a journey or a ride I was on during tough times. They kept my mind active, distracted, and focused. They gave me a way to take hard things, and try to say them in beautiful, interesting, and creative ways. I guess they were an outlet for me to plug into when things were chaotic.

My writing has always been precious to me, and here, it sits open and on display. This collection chokes me up every damn time I read it. Because it's me, *I Am My Words Here*; and I'm not sure I know exactly how to welcome you to that—but welcome all the same!

When I was little, I wanted to be a songwriter. I wanted to move to Nashville and live a musician's life—out on the road, traveling around, and writing music with the greats. I have always been deeply inspired by the art of music—specifically, that therapy you find in the sound and lyrics on the days you really need them. In 1987, I was six years old and for Christmas, I got a Mickey Mouse cassette player with a microphone. I also got a K.T. Oslin tape, and I remember listening to *Hey Bobby* and *Hold Me* about a zillion times and imagining what it would feel like to be the protagonist—live the song. My imagination was magic as a child, and it still lives and breathes in me today!

There's absolutely nothing more satisfying to me than finding new music, connecting with it, and adding it to my very exclusive and very private 'My Guts' playlist! Music inspires me every single day, and sometimes, gets me through the night. (Most nights actually!)

In college, I dove into literature unexpectedly. I remember my dad giving me side-eye when I told him I was changing my major to English—in hindsight, I guess it worked out well for me! I added hundreds of classic novels, short stories, and poems to my repertoire at Radford University. Like music, I clung to writers or artists who were bold, with interesting perspectives and interesting ways of saying old things.

If there ever was a work that changed my perspective or inspired me as a human, it would be *The Ones Who Walk Away from Omelas*, by Ursula K. LeGuin, or equally as monumental, Janis Joplin's Cry Baby—both for very different reasons. These stories run so desperately deep inside me. They shaped me, and I think you'll find similar themes in my own writing—or at least several references to them. I bow before their artistry, and thank them for their influence on mine.

So many people, places, and songs inspired this collection. You will find me going through many highs and lows here, but there's nothing more real or true—words that I believe in. I hope you can find pieces of yourself in my work and relate; that would be my biggest triumph of all.

Poetry is magic.

I find that poetry, like art, adds color to a world that is linear, logical, and mathematical. It fills in gaps of space just like air—if you are open, in tune, and creative enough to absorb it. I think when I needed it the most; I met someone who reminded me to nurture the seismic activity inside me, and to pull it out for the world to see. He made me believe that anything is possible. Just to reach for it, and speak it—most of all, *master time, relentlessly design, and work like hell until you unwind.*

To the very elusive *Shape-Shifting Escapist*, thank you for the being you helped me become—literarily unafraid.

I'm already writing a second collection to share, and I find myself in a different headspace entirely. Life is interesting that way. There's a line in one of these poems I wrote about "*just waiting for circumstances to change*", and they certainly have. They aren't what I thought I wanted at the time, but I'm grateful for my past, present, and future me. I believe in her, *religiously*!

I appreciate you for reading along and supporting me! I'm more grateful than words can say—but hopefully, I'll get close and you'll feel it in the pages ahead. You are a gift. Thank you!

Cheers!

If You Fall

If you fall
Fall with me

Into madness and pure insanity
Where life waits
And emotion is just curated
Into art for the rest of the world to see
Isn't that what everyone really needs
Some construct that we're all free
With the safety of complete anonymity
No fence, without any consequence
Just the ability to fall
Yet still have it all

If you fall
Fall with me

Inspiration

You're a firecracker
Popping in the sky
Feathers free falling
A lone wolf's cry

You're a sky light
With a glimpse of the sun
A Bob Dylan song
Before it's even begun

You're an intense feeling
So deep, so serene
You're my blank piece of paper
Water-colored floral, mountain scene

You're the times I feel like crying
A long romantic stare
Red Rocks and Lady Gaga
Feeling high without a care

Inspiration, you always find me
Pencil in hand
Words fall effortlessly on paper
So simple, yet so grand

Together, we'll write poems
Let the world in, let them see
The beauty, angst, and chaos
That live inside of me

Utopia

Utopia is you
You are me
An image, a muse, an unfortunate love story

Or maybe some beautiful excuse
Inspired, set free
Not you, me—it's tomfoolery

With absolute precision and care
I just set you right there
And I stare

I wonder and long for grandeur
But it's not there
It's beyond repair—and I can't find air, anywhere

Utopia is you
But you are me
Emotionally distressed—but rediscovering my artistry

Subpar Poetry

Who am I? Who are we?
Just words in subpar poetry?

Some days I forget none of this is real
Some days I forget it's just not that big of a deal

It was something and nothing, wrapped in box and bow
It was hearts-in-a-circle around my neck, then we let it go

Yet, you remain here, so close/so far away
I trudge through these emotions every single day

Who am I? Who are we?
Just words in subpar poetry?

Find Me

Find me when you shut your eyes and
when you cannot breathe
Find me when you're tired and
when you're ready to leave
Find me when you're weak there and
love has done you wrong
Find me when you're driving in a
sunset or a song
Find me when you wake
with zest and energy
Find me when you're running wild and
when you're feeling free
Find me on the dark days too
when hope is nowhere near
Find me when you're dreaming and
the future seems so clear
Find me when you're confused and
question right or wrong
And find me when you lay there in your bed
overthinking all day long
Find me when you're playful
when you laugh at something new
Find me when you're scared of change and

don't know what to do
Find me when you have an idea
on the verge of some breakthrough
Find me when you're lonely and
just need to feel something true

Find me lost out on the road or
find my soul renewed
No matter how you find me, find me
you know I'll always love you

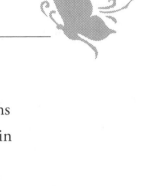

Wednesday Whitman

Let's get philosophical with fine wine
And solve the world's most complex problems
Recite Whitman on a Wednesday metro train
With the lamest-of-lame champagne
Because really, it's all the same
And while today, we cheers as champions of the "Can You
Remember the Singer's Name" game,
Tomorrow, you're on the next plane
And I'll still be here, riding out this mundane

Can You Hear Me

Do you have the ability to hear me
Take this and dance off the page
Are we in sync here and are you phased
Can we get to the next level, next stage

It depends
If you can actually hear me

To Make You Like Me

I don't need you to like me

Just "like me" here

In a forum

Where pictures, that aren't real

Do all the talking

And words that rhyme

Live on a page with strangers for all time

To no one's surprise

It's all just lies

But we still vibe…and I try

To make you like me

Purgatory

The yelling became white noise
And brazenness destroyed
The harmony of the house
It became ruthless without a doubt
And they walked around on egg shells
It was years of trying to defend them
And from the outside looking in
An overall waste of energy
They were all tired
Of living their lives on fire
And one day they started to ask "why?"
Tired of living some elaborate lie
And ready to feel some kind of peace
In a house that wasn't Purgatory
And with people that felt more like family

Feel the Mountain

You can't feel the mountain under your feet
The magnitude escapes us, as you race to fleet

I'm standing here wild, inviting you in
But you can't feel the mountain under your skin

Everything falls quiet, in the still of the night
You hear the same silence, and almost miss your next flight

Real life chaos and we're back at the start
Because you can't feel the mountain down deep in your heart

Next Day Adventure

Next Day Adventure is a comical thing
Words profound, words that actually sting
It's honesty that reigns supreme
A writer unleashed, just livin' a dream
It's words unspoken, spoken
My dead-become-living, spirit evokin'
On my Next Day Adventure

Some nights, I go to a real special place
Stare down my cares, directly in their face
And tell my sweet little truth, "it's fine"
In fact, she and I cheers with wine
Send a big F-You
To nights feeling blue
And we ride that Next Day Adventure

This pad and me, we're a dynamic two
Let's just see what we can construe
We've been here together night-after-night
Writing poems, talkin' 'bout "we'll be all right"
Creating masterpiece shit
Breaking me down bit-by-bit
For my Next Day Adventure

Words She'd Never Keep

She wrote poems on a Monday night
Just her, Pink Floyd, Vodka, and Sprite
And everything flowed kinda slow
And everything was just all right

Some moments she got incredibly deep
But more so, just dingy, drunk, and cheap
And none of it mattered
They were just rogue words

Words she'd never keep

Out of the Dark

Transpose it, make it real
The words are here to reveal what I conceal

I bet I wasn't a victim in your mind
I bet my energy misled you—because "she's so happy, so kind!"

Now it's here for you, to devour and stare
Dare I expose it? Do I care?

Truth is, this is just me
On a path to discovery…or maybe even some kind of recovery

On some spiritual mission to re-believe
Or better yet, find some kind of sanity…through this poetry

It's All Undone

It's the story no one wants to hear
When the rock bottom they already knew
Just hit you—and silently, you're just choking on the truth
Pretending to be absolutely bulletproof and unshaken
It's the long days they don't see
When drinks become puddle and fumes
And a haze erases all the days
All just blurred into one—it's some pain, some fun

But truth is, it's all undone

Reality

Oh blessed human endeavor
Look @ reality so cunning and clever
Twist of fate; sad and blue
Delivered; then it fell right through

17

Time Master

Master of design
Superpower: Time
But only a smoke-filled room, an illusion
All about to unwind

I see you trying, ticking
Relentless, to manage it all
It's tedious, it's unfair
But you do it with the utmost care

In one instance, time stood still
We lifted off-the-ground, were upside down
You said the word "scared"
Lapsed in the moment, recoiled

Master repaired

And, over-and-over again still…

You are the master of time
Relentlessly, you design
And you work like hell
But it's all about to unwind

The Truth

I've always been honest
Said exactly what I felt
Until my words hurt you
And I saw the blow it dealt

Now I manage your emotions
Before I speak a word
Fall silent when you ask for clarification
Regarding what you just heard

It's much easier for me to ignore
The feelings you feel
If I don't acknowledge them
They aren't real

Galaxy Crack

Red-eyed whimsy
Drunk as can be
I stumbled on warmth
So cold and contradictory
Here, but gone
Silent, but loud
I can't find your heart here
Alone in this crowd

You're not the same now
Quiet—unapologetically lame
It's like I barely know you
Like we're playing some lethargic game
I fight to preserve it
Keep the beauty on track
But the magic escaped us
Through a galaxy crack

My Country Road

My country road
An endless path of bent trees

Feeling the softness of a gentle summer breeze
Longing for reprieve…for you and for me
Or to maybe just feel free

Time tapers the feeling though
And truth speaks like a giant…dead freakin' silent

The mountains stand regal and strong
A backdrop proud
And the answer is loud

Don McLean Starry Night

Mom said the point was that he wrote about van Gogh
And even just at mentally so-so
His art inspired art
That if you look long enough
At Starry, Starry Night
You too might fall apart
Because life's not simple
It is not pristine
Doesn't run like any ole machine
It's just an impressionist's dream
Blurry and unclean
Which I guess, is the real masterpiece
There's nothing ordinary—only extraordinary
When you live your best Starry, Starry life

Watcher of Dark Things

Watcher of dark things,
What could you possibly see?
Does my silence tell you some illuminated story?
Is there ever really glory?

And just where does that leave me?

Watcher of dark things,
Is the long night there also lonely?
Are you ever scared to face the light?
Will it inevitably be all right?

I feel a bit unsettled and unruly.

Watcher of dark things,
How do you find your peace,
When you see all the things you see?
Are you scared when you look upon me, a reflection of humanity?

House of Mirrors

I was ashamed of all that we'd become
Kept it behind closed doors
What I didn't realize was
We lived in a house of ~~horrors~~ mirrors
A house of everyday lies, to absolutely no one's surprise
The truth was reflected every which way we turned
And we didn't even know it

People could see through us
Every angle, every turret, every turn
They saw through the disguise
Right through us—right through what we could become

And when we fell apart
It was crystal clear why
They didn't bat one single eye
Because our walls revealed it all
That hopeful ascension, rappelling from a wall
And then our embarrassing, monumental fall
They saw every bit of it—they saw it all

Absolutely Everywhere

She was falling down deep
Into a charade, she could no longer keep up with
And loss was absolutely everywhere

She tried to pretend she didn't care
But the truth lingered in the air
It was absolutely everywhere

She took long walks
To get a minute alone, but the second she came home
The truth was absolutely, devastatingly everywhere

The Pain Won't Last

Slain self
Victim, bruised
Broken down
Hurt, abused
Hardly breathing
Tired, torn
Lay there sad
Battered, worn
Restlessly silent
The past is the past
Stand and move forward
The pain, it won't last

Move On Selfishly

Monster dark and deadly
Stuck living in your head
I want so bad to save you from it
Breathe life into you, dead
But you forsake me every minute
Turn your back, say you don't care
"We don't have a future"
You say—but that just isn't fair
Inside, I know you love me
But that disease won't let you live
So you turn your back and hurt me
Not a kindness left to give
After months of desperation
You come back for a glimpse of me
Tell me I have nice legs
And move on selfishly

Friday Dinner Date

You kinda messed up my equilibrium
Left me here spinning around
I sat here writing poems
To help me stand firm on the ground

Among the architecture
Of a beautifully constructed word
I pieced together our story
With a future, uncertain and blurred

Amidst the art of my writing
You came back in flesh and in bone
We sat down to a dinner awkward
Beside you, I felt cold and alone

You, as a man, are fickle
You are simply complicated as can be
And on this messed up journey
You failed to take care of me

Now I'm writing this all like a victim
A casualty in the game of you
But the art, it freakin' healed me
Like poetry will often do

Just Friends

I noticed you didn't see me
When you glanced quickly at my eyes
My depth and all my beauty
And that adoration for you, I simply despise

We sat fumbling through the basics
A dinner stripped of poetic truth
I wanted so bad to kiss you
But sat paralyzed right there in the booth

Where and when did love evade us?
How did you lose sight of me so quick?
You describe me now as your rebound
Good love and an open heart really did the trick

You ask me where this leaves me
You ask about somebody new
You ask if I'm okay now
Am I really okay without you?

The answer to all of those questions
I'm trying so hard to find
My feelings are still intact here
You're still floating around in my mind

I'm certain I can move on now
Okay with your abrupt, cinematic end
But it's hard to let go of a future together
When you're so much more than my friend

Breaking Up

In the mutterings of "it has to be"
I assure you "I'll be fine"
"I love you but I understand"
Is always my go-to tagline

How do we remain friends?
I really don't know what to do
In the playbook of messed up love
Is this something we all have to go through?

Roots

Roots
Who exactly are you
But a mystery to me
You're woven blankets through time
Tattered, torn
And lost, only to find later
When your mind
Opens
At the age
When you want to know
Where you're from
But more so
To plant roots
For your very own
So they know
Who they are
Who we are
Who we all once were
And we can cover up
With what we've all sewn
Our homegrown
Woven blankets
Of our very own

Snapshots

Passerby
Come or go
On or off
Rain or snow
Life moves
Snapshots fall
In piles
Of forgotten thoughts

South Beach Vibes

Read like you're me
See my heart here--in these four counts
Shot of Jose
Picture on the wall
Just says it all
Nude and exposed
But fully clothed
I'm in here, breathing
And oh the vibes
Made me come alive
Inspiration
Right here, revived

Swept Away

Listen to what's down there
Declutter, break down the mind
Stand tall against the darkness
Whisper calmly, "It's just fine"

The darkness overwhelms it
Grips me while I gasp
Murmurs of feeling scared there
Succumb to pain's momentous blast

For a moment, I thought that I loved you
Small grin, romantic glare
So quickly, we fell silent
Disappeared right into thin air

The future washed away
Like waves there on the shore
Remnants of what used to be
Swept away and gone—no more

Just Go

The world is out there
For you to *just go*
Out there, it's just what's next
Your job/Your life
Goes on-and-on

The world is out there
For me to *just go*
Right here; build, learn, grow
My job/My life
Goes on-and-on

Our worlds don't seem to collide
Never prescribed
So we part, almost as quick as we start
And the world goes on-and-on

Just Isn't Me

We jumped right in, didn't we?
Full-fledged, free
Our imaginations wild→living recklessly

Can't have it all, can we?
You showed me a glimpse of happy
Then, tank→empty

One more leap into the space between doubt and fantasy
We're tangled and troubled—wild, lucid frenzy
And it just isn't me→just isn't me

Tennessee Wisdom

Some man with some wisdom

Pacing the Tennessee streets

Greeting people on the crosswalk of dreams

One he tells to stop; one he tells to go slow

While the passerbys come, and inevitably go

He stays there, ready to greet them

With nothing but a friendly face, and some wisdom

The only thing he has to give them

Count Me In

Count me in
Not just for the win
But for the rumble

I'll be your sidekick
Your GO-TO chick
For that wild unknown—cause you ain't alone

You can count me in

No Super Mom

Someone said today
Not being a perfect mom was just freakin' okay
Because super moms can't, and don't, do it all
And when life beats them down,
They don't fall
They simply crawl
Or simply stand tall

And their best is good enough

Someone said today
That perfect was only an illusion
And joy was the only conclusion
So stop driving so hard to the baseline
Stop obsessing about your waistline
And the work you accomplished today was just fine
Have that glass of wine

Because your best is good enough

Nomad Roam

Thank God for the road to nowhere
And the air of feeling wild and free
We rode down Old Route 66 in a Dodge Charger—livin' our lives at full speed
After a night in Vegas, we slept on Dana Point concrete
I listened all night to Passenger, Lumineers, and Amos Lee—on an epic repeat

We drove the El Camino Real
Slept with that Pacific Ocean view
I was thinking it was so surreal all night too
Some feeling no one ever freakin' knew
Instead of a pinch, we stopped the next day in Encinitas for some random ass tattoos
Just so we knew it was all true
And not some California daydream, a Vegas mirage, or a story we misconstrued (after way too much booze)

And it was so freakin' cool
And it was so freakin' new
Just me and you
Doin' what besties do
Out on our road to nowhere

We rode the Pacific Coast Highway, down the coast

Only stopping at hole-in-the-walls that intrigued our hearts the most

We threw up our hands for the awesomest bands

And we threw down shots to forget our real world grind—and what was behind

It was solely about having the windows down, feeling the sun and the sound

Taking in every single thing around—Arizona bound

A few silent days, without a single care

And just because we both needed the rejuvenation, some fresh air

Even though we both had a precious home

For a few drawn out days, we did some kind of nomad roam

And it was revolutionary in a way

Because of how we got lost in a day—and with nothing more than a spirit of adventure

Together, for a moment

We were free

-For April

Fumes of Lost Time

The fumes of lost time
Fog up my view
Out here with questions
"Where are you?"

Tedious inquiry
Meaning that's true
Random messages pop up
"I love you"

Sit here in silence
Life in review
What are we doing?
"I just miss/hate you"

Muse Hall Fall

That unhinged elevator
In Muse Hall
Plummets
Drops
It just falls
Right out
Of the sky

I wince
I panic
I cry

Dreams
Where I
Perpetually die
A thousand times
With a heart
That still beats
Rhythmically wild
Inside an inner child
With her silent voice

In this silent place
In this silent space

Where questions lie wide-awake

My reason
My purpose
My desires

Looking for any sign
I can possibly find
In the dark art
Of my
Subliminal mind

Some Days

Some days I hate you
For dragging me out
Weak and fragile
Full of doubt

Sitting here waiting
For a call or a text
Telling myself, you gone
Is probably what's next

Most days I love you
True and complete
Finding fault
In everyone else that I meet

What is love though
A test of the mind
Back and forth
Ahead, but behind

The On-Going Game

You just can't have it
The torment that came
From waiting around
For circumstances to change

The wait and the pain
Made me kind of insane
But I laid there excited to keep playing
The on-going game

"It's Just You"

Downtime daydreams
That "I'm so sorry" overdue
I just can't shake you
Even though it wasn't true

I defend you when I'm questioned
All your mixed messages too
I tell them that you're hurt and broken
I tell them "it's just you"

Turn Around

Clung to it
Said a prayer
Wished everyday
You'd be there
And some days, you were there
But dreams aren't enough
I need you to love me
And this silence is rough

I hope one day, you'll stop
Perhaps you'll turn around
Come back here to me
Stake your feet here in the ground

Shape-Shifting Escapist

Shape-shifting escapist
Released into the world
In a million faceless people
You relentlessly explore

You're lost among the masses
Lost inside of you
A complex identity matrix
With no real inner truth

You live life like a movie
Hopping around scene-to-scene
Your life of romantic ambiguity
Detracts from any daily routine

But it captivates you, and you run
Striving so hard just to make it
The truth is on your coattails now
And it's getting harder-and-harder to fake it

Too Much

There's just so much
Too much
Responsibility
For me

There's just so much
Too much
You & me
Realistically

What's so much
Too much
At the cost
Of happy?

Patterns

Down in doubt, feeble in fear
　　Searching for love in anyone near

It pours from a bottle, pencil in hand
　　Gobs of attention, but not the right man

Your back faces me, far, far away
　　Okay with silence, with not much to say

I long for connection, indications of hope
　　Inhale and hold it, but nearly choke

Your eyes dance around, so playful and fun
　　You reappear smiling; I know we're not done

My heart finds relief in the words that you say
　　But the pattern's familiar, you're gone the next day

Nowhere Street

How do you untangle love
Feelings so complete
I want you,
I need you,
You make my heart beat

Your eyes are so compelling
Tell a story of deceit
I want you,
I need you,
Here on Nowhere Street

Loose Cannon Here

I'm no master of words
In fact, I'm just a loose cannon here
One hot mess, spilling and dumping
My feelings on paper
Sometimes turning them into songs
Fumbling through them all night long
With candles—and a better sense of self

It's amazing, my red-eyed flights
Through turbulent and unnerving times
Journeys of an unresolved mind
Seeking solitude
Or maybe some high
That kind of honesty that only requires
Masterful attention, this old guitar, and these stars

A Thought

I don't have much to say today, but "HEY!"
I'm lost in my own corridor of horror, mind-war
With "what's next?" questions pressing on my chest
Ambition second-guessed

While I pace through the processes "I need"
That ultimately define me
Silence is hard to find in a grind
Where creativity is utterly left behind

Tasks scuffle to find absolution in a world
Of endless priorities, where people never sleep
And 9-to-5 zombies, with rampant insecurities
Mindlessly disbelieve in possibility

Every step forward is a bit more,
But to what accord?
I'm just here bored in my very core
And sometimes, that's hard to ignore

Shades of Blue

You are tattooed, drunken stars
Slouched on a navy-painted canvas
And I am in awe of your craft

I am the little pastel blue version of you
With only these words that tell a story

-For My Mom

It's Messy

Isn't it heavy?
Isn't it messy?
Isn't this all just down-dirty depressing?

Like a salad
Without the Caesar dressing
And a sky
Without blue
A 2020 stew
Of just missing you

And it's heavy
And it's messy
It's down-right dirty depressing

Sunsets

It's not all good
It's yellows and blues
Lost in a sunset
That's really a bruise
The red grabs you
With its elegant hues
The heat pulls you in
And the mountain consumes

That West Virginia Night Sky

Imagine me there
Look up at that West Virginia night sky
In all its glory, the stars tell a billion stories
But none quite as brilliant as ours
Imagine us laughing
On my parent's porch, rocking
Fumbling through words
Reminiscing over moments forgotten
Imagine us there hand-in-hand, eye-to-eye
Campfire flaming wild
Charcuterie board style
Talking about life—as lovers and friends
It's Almost Heaven again-and-again
Our beginning and our end
Right there, look up at that West Virginia night sky

West Virginia Writing

Justice-in-words just isn't served
for that West Virginia sunset

Mountains get high, when suns sink in their sky
and skylines die for their love of the night

Imagine me, sitting under this big Oak tree
by her Campfire Majesty, writing enchantedly

While those stars shine in Moonshine Wine
and I resign, to find the time to make love to each and every line

61

Unclench

How hard can you clench
To hold in what's about
To come rushing out
Released in a stream
Of words, a scream of words
A final act, a display
And a few drinks at the end of a hard day
That really didn't end pretty

You look around, and aren't feeling so proud
Because this, it's cosmically loud
And you're spent
And now they are all dead silent
It's all a little broken, but decently well-spoken
Even if it's gaping and hanging grossly open
Like an old garden gate

Sitting unhinged and lifeless there
Opening and closing with the air
Creaking more-and-more with passing time
In some unintentional rhyme
That you often find
Healthy for an unresolved mind
Even though someone called it "hard to swallow"

This is just your outlet, a conduit
To escape reality, to rest and sit
And find a way to heal
A way to get in there again, and simply feel
Again, finally just let it all go
Let it all flow
Unclench

Faith

Nobody knew the truth
But they professed to know
So much so
They would wake up early just to go
And they preached a gospel
And threw their money in a bowl
And people listened...
They offered up their heart and soul

For something nobody knew

They studied an ancient book
To feel far less removed
From their very existence
They'd talk about concepts like faith and grace
And an afterlife place
Where you'd finally see "his" glory
Really, an exquisite story...
Of peace

And nobody knew the truth

But they'd close their eyes and pray
Every single day

Sing the Lord's song
To keep the faith strong
And for those that questioned
Or had been through complete hell
They would quell their sorrows and fear…
Let them know there was a holy spirit near

Even though nobody knew the truth

Falling

I tried so hard to get to the top of the mountain
But it was the plunge off the edge that really saved me
And they said "pick yourself up" and I wanted to
I was trying to do all that I could do
But I jumped off anyway

I'm still here with Petty....free falling
Day-after-day-after-day
Falling

3:41

Wander with me, without purpose aimlessly

I'll be around, man—livin' free

It was that one line that got me—*"I mean, really!"*

It's the stop button on old dreams

And the start button on the new

A realization that you don't really know what to do

But your heart finally wins

And you *Cry Baby*—then allow yourself to re-begin

This time with a purpose

That fried chicken, a blanket of fur

And of course, with her

-For Janis

The Pack

Phenomenally, she led the pack
Phenomenally, they grew
And when dark days approached them all
They were equipped to do what they had to do

She taught them to rely on their instincts
But hold tight to each other like glue
And when they felt scared she came back
Just so they felt something true

-For Carolyn

Not a Man

You're not a man, you're a mountain
A geographical work of art
You stand tall and proud with honor
Yet remain humble and share your heart

You're not a man, you're an eagle
Flying majestic and strong
Providing for your family
Working hard all year long

You're not a man, you're a painting
Fine lines, so abstract
Watercolors of emotion
On a canvas, so exact

You're not a man, you're a poem
Words scrawled strategically on a page
Scribbled with deep meaning
Written in beauty and rage

You're not a man, you're our man
We appreciate you every day
You're a miracle God gave us
And that is all I have to say

The Hustle

It's all an upward spiral
Or so that's what they say
You work hard to build something
Not to just piss it all away

And I am not just some ivy
Standing tall within the league
I'm a single, working mama
Hustlin' magic to succeed

Among black suits of business
Thoughts run wild in my brain
Up all night working
Creativity insane

Innovate, innovate
The world is yours to recreate
Fluctuate, fluctuate
Diversify, differentiate

Hustle, hustle
Fight to win
Focus on outcomes
Before you even begin

They'll poke and prod
To get to the ideas inside your mind
Judging your talent
Capitalizing on any good one they can find

Work hard and keep going
Withstand the bumps and whoa
See how far the corporation
Will invest and let you go

Or STOP…take in the silence
Listen…and veer off course
Let your mind and body rest
Revive your spiritual life force

Be mindful of the future
Your desires and your needs
Intentionally craft a master plan
That truly helps you succeed

What if life's not about the hustle
It's not about the climb
Just enjoy every minute
Be mindful, maximize your time

Shadow of Doubt

Shadow of doubt, come out!
Let's talk sensibly about the future

A million lies will compromise
The many great things before you

Stop tapping the brakes, weighing the stakes
And open your heart to possibility

Who knows what you can do
When you just believe in you

I Am My Words Here

I am my words here
Every single one
Thoughts undone

I am a thousand unopened letters
Words left unspoken
Poetry, heartbroken

I am my words here

Without the Rain

This old bucket sat on its stoop
Reminiscent of days shiny,
Red and blue
And now, no one really knew it was there feeling empty

Day-after-day
It sat and it craved the rain
Which sounds so insane
That it chose the rust over a little dust

But no one was ever around
And desperately, it just needed to drown
Tip over, fall down
Roll

It needed to feel out-of-control
And to ride the wind
Because sitting there, without a friend
It frankly, had lost its purpose

It felt absolutely worthless
Just a bucket of pain
Without any rain
Which sounds so insane

Something New

Like a vulture
I circled it
Picked it apart

Ate at my own broken heart

Until it became desperate, desperate art
And eventually, my new start

Scheme of Me

I've toiled over you
Hell bent to find truth
But it will never come
And maybe that's okay
Because your side
Really doesn't matter
In the scheme
Of me

Dreams

It was obscure, and almost a missed opportunity
But they met, reconciling fairy tales
And designing dreams

Dreams that would never happen
But that really felt good to believe

Even if for only a second
And even if only a memory

Didn't Matter

10,000 reasons
10,000 words
Left undisturbed
And unsaid

Truth was
She was dead
And the things in her head
Didn't matter

The Lost and Found

Maybe we found it
Dragged it out of its hole
Resuscitated emotions
Beyond our control

Perhaps we found it
Living in fear
Clouded with doubt
But almost crystal clear

I think we found it
Swept us off our feet
Together we were brilliant
Beautiful and sweet

What if we lost it?
Because we couldn't commit
Tossed it in the air
Probably just easier to quit

We definitely lost it
Hands in the air
You can't force love
You can't make it care

The Letters

I carry around these letters
To places without faces
Where people have no name
And I look upon them often
Feeling exactly the same

Obsolete

We weren't just friends
We were chapters
Of a story wildly incomplete

We were love in perilous free fall
Then closed off
And buried deep

We were silent for a moment
Then deafened
By defeat

We let the silence settle
The 'us' disappeared
Obsolete

Certainty Uncertain

A decent offer lies rejected on the table
As a slow blues song buzzes into the grey-background-
music-of-the-day
It's "a relationship that no longer makes sense"—and she's wounded
and feels thrown away

Logic taps its foot impatiently, pointing at an exit door
With no hesitation, she lays the rest of her cards on the table and
waits there, hopeful
His brow sits puzzled looking at a future of certainty—but still
so uncertain

And with the echo of a "no", time peddled forward with absolutely
no absolution—and old feelings pause right there ageless, haggard,
and silent

Glimpses of their past sparkle like stars on dreary, lifeless nights—
and they can almost feel the other there

Children laugh on a summer day, water splashes, and happiness
is a warm daydream—although, he can't help but miss the way
they'd also play

Somewhere thousands of miles away, she looks out the window watching an orange sun's glory fade effortlessly into pastels—she wonders if he sees it, if like her, he needs it….if he believes in it

Fate chuckles a little as memories evoke curiosity--curiosity makes a quick call

After all this time the answer is finally "yes"

Uncertainty

Built me up
To take me down
Afraid to let the truth
Crumble me to the ground
Instead, uncertainty dealt the blow
I laid in the rubble
God, I felt so low

The Lesson

You opened your heart
Then slammed the door
Twice more for sport
Until I hit the floor

I call you my lesson
One we all have to learn
To hold yourself back
Where love is concerned

Truth, Styled by You

I see you here
Quietly, trying to find you

She told me it would be better to tell a story
Without actually using the real words
Put it in a game of Hide-and-Seek, play
And leave you all guessing
And leave 'me' as an ambiguous kind-of question
And so I laid it down, I wrote
Tilt-a-Whirled some kind of truth for you
Into a story
With absolutely no proof
And I used dark and light
And day and night
And metaphors to make wrong feel alright
It was all just a mystery
Mixed with straight history
All just words on paper—allegory
And when they read it, they all tried
And those close to her, they all cried
And some of them probably thought she lied
But here, there's no such thing as solitary truth

The truth was always just styled by you
And this, it's just what we've both been through

Trust in the Feeling

Standing on the edge of a decision
With absolutely no reprieve
Nowhere to go now
But to the future full speed

Bury the past
Or let it fly away free
Trust in the feeling
Religiously

Blank Page

I bet you are critiquing as you read this
Sizing up the sentiment and slowly settling in somewhere between safe and uncertain
Dusting me off like some old antique sitting in a side shop, with my sold sign—by eternal design

Fine wine and good old times saturate the free flow of forgotten friendship
Sad songs play now on a playlist repeated, and feelings fall freely from eyes so damn surprised

Up there, stars still stand in the night reaching for 'the dream'—their dream
Some obscurity they started writing with words of whimsy in Washington D.C.—with a single penny thrown into a fountain of fortune

And now, memories like majestic monuments stand tall there—just pages staggering around stark, with not a hint of dark or a single mark

Lost; a dream faded beyond recognition into a background of weathered, white walls

The wasteland-of-their-wrong-doing reminds him of winters and her waiting, and her writing, and her wanting what he could not give her

He was just the ultimate abyss of assailed ambition—unwavering apprehension abound, which took them both to the ground without a single sound

And in memories from-then-on, they would always be a blank page—poetry assuaged and left unwritten

Grandest Gesture

It was maybe the grandest gesture of all

Letting it go

Letting the cards fall

Letting our creative energies expand and evolve

Into some old, sad song

Stacked up there on the shelf for too long

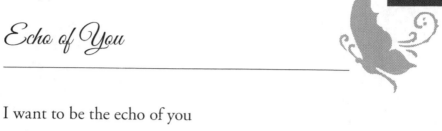

Echo of You

I want to be the echo of you
Help you remember
What we've been through
And where we came from
I want to be everything
Of value
Of importance
Everything that rings true
And when you see Mirrors
Our Mountain Mama
Old photos of you
I hope you see me there too
Looking right back at you
And deep in your heart
You hear
The echo of you

Hurry Up and Wait

Hurry up and wait,
Wait for me to find me
I'm out here in the world,
Pretending to be carefree

Heaven-By-Design

What if Heaven is somewhere deep inside your mind
A neurological masterpiece by your very own design
Behind all the things you could ever possibly know
Beyond where science will ever let you go
And your soul is just the place your mind finds
When you literally implode down into you
Into the afterlife foretold
Your very own yellow brick road

And along the way, you see galaxies, stars
In some film'esque display; everyday it's all replayed
And you can finally reconcile the who's-who inside you
Find the people you always knew
To re-live memories
For centuries and centuries
Without time, without gravity
In some beautiful parade of simple relativity

It's all unique to you, and to what you manifest to be true
It's all inside your mind, refined
It's Heaven-by-design

Broken

The "all in" was lies
While a million silent "whys?"
I left unspoken

You were my demise
One hell of a surprise
And I just sat there broken

Extraction Day

Please tell me tomorrow isn't here already
And that I have more time to think—and drink
I'm not ready to be brave—Nope, not yet
I still need to play *Til I Collapse* on repeat
And find some inner peace
Alas, I blink and it's that time to rise, shine
Eyes closed tight, I cross the dreaded line

A World Gone Askew

Stale stage
Average grey, everyday
A need to find peace
In a world
Gone askew

It's dreary
Solemn 'To Dos'
Nothing ever new
More of the same, outrage
Fatigue

Just trying to make it through
Daily downers
And to find a reason to move
Get up, go
Breathe

To finally see
Beauty
In this beast
Of a world
Gone askew

Privilege

I noticed the flow of the free folk
The perpetual need for a beat
I found the frontline formation
From a particularly formidable seat
I watched as the people passed by me
Looking so scared and alone
I decide to join their formation
March into the dark and unknown
Today, I look back on endeavors
Proud that I rallied for peace
Cause free folk ain't free folk in silence
And the future needs people to teach

Apple in Peanut Butter Night

What an 'Apple in Peanut Butter Night' I have here
Laying in bed
Scrollin' a thread
Just shakin' my silly ole head

And laughing—because I'm just so dead!

And it makes no sense
And I love it that way
Just the right way to end my day
With an 'Apple in Peanut Butter Night'

Stupid Ole Me

You look at me with disgust
When I tell you that story's about you
Embarrassed, you tell me "I'm Stupid!"
And I shrug, because I've already spoken
I guess it's hard to hear you're broken

Even from Stupid Ole Me

Warrior Art

She sat down on a top-of-the-line mower—he bought
And looked out
At five scorned acres of tall weeds,
Pine trees, and wayward grass—kinda resembled me
Once a field of her dreams
Now, long gone and unachieved
It was simply-and-complexly overgrown
And they told her just not to cut it
"That's probably not the right machine"
But that day, like so many lately
She rode the lines recklessly—at demon speed
Plaid pattern by her own drunken design
Listening to Em's Recovery—ironically
Line-by-sad-ass-line

She got stuck
Revved it all back up
And pressed on, like absolute fire and absolute hell
Stung by bees, cut by branches on trees
Covered in sap, cut grass, crap, and spilled Chablis
But she'd made up her mind, she'd ride-or-die before she'd bend
the knee
Mostly because she was mixed up

With something to prove
She was a pissed off woman—
And a warrior by day
And something sad—
A broken piece of art at night
And over-and-over again
This was her life

Until one day, she decided it wasn't!

Hope

Do you wonder if a single, solitary prayer
Can make a difference
In the world and out in the air
What if we all, together
Can create some colossal change
Even through some arbitrary, single exchange
Of simple faith

Why wouldn't we try?
Why wouldn't we break down, cry
To help?

Let's be the definition of hope
Believe in more than just science
Or scope
And just lift the things up we can't carry
Send up a prayer
Just for God to be there
Because it's all we can

It's the end of what we understand
Just an open heart, our hands, and
Hope

Bet

Bet

Bet I can stay silent longer

Bet

Bet I can pretend to not care

Bet I can shake you up, then disappear into thin air

Bet

Bet I can make you jealous

Bet I can come back again

Bet I can lead you on

Bet you'll never win

Bet

Drink Before the Cheers

We'll always be this way:
I forget and drink before the cheers

And you:
Well, you judge me for it

The Punchline

The words she so desperately wanted to hear
Were stuck in his anticipation
Playing there, in his head on repeat
For a while, they stumbled around the truth
Laughed and drank wine
And instead of letting his words fly
The punchline was simply her time

Love Like Never Before

Depreciated you

Broken, misused

Emotionally bruised

Scared, confused

Come out from behind the door!

Lies and hurt, no more

You've been through one hell of a war

Now, let me love you like never before

The Façade

The façade we live
It's comfort
It's safe
It's space
Yet, we all ignore
The things no one actually wants to say
The buried
The misplaced
What's here
What's all over the place
Because it's hard to face

The facade

2 A.M. Musings

My 2 a.m. poems don't lie
They are dead dreams—make me cry
Relentless and raw
Like every single sad story I ever saw

And it keeps me awake at night

Your 2 a.m. poems are unequivocally you
They are everything, absolutely true
Dreams finally spoken out loud; in front of a stadium-sized crowd
The dreams you said "make you proud"

And it helps you sleep at night

All the Bad Times We Simply Forgot

I laughed that day and finally let go
Of a thousand bad days before you
You shined the brightest in my eyes—
were a beautiful surprise
And so different than what I was used to

And every day since the first one
We've wound ourselves in a tight knot
Walking together side-by-side—
in a perfect stride
And all the bad times, we simply forgot

-For Edwin

Proud

I walk through the new with you
And the life you gave my ambitions
I write because you called my work brilliant
And you looked at me like you were proud

I can take the next step confidently
Because even though I feel weak
I know you really truly believe in me
And that's all I really need

Creative Little Moments

She played with words at night
Mainly to digest her life
Into creative little moments

Each piece, she'd own it
Then poetically condone it
Flipping her color to a nostalgic black-and-white

Hard Getting Old

"Amanda Jayne, it's hard getting old!"
She'd say bold—with her certain conviction
And truth was, we all knew it
Old age was perhaps the worst-of-the-worst cage
And we hadn't even begun to really go through it

"Life happens at warp speed", she'd concede
And she can't begin to believe she's in her 80's—
with those two sore knees
And maybe a tad out of touch with reality—
or so she believes

Trapped inside a faulty mind, a tad blind
And lost in a shuffle of a whole new time
She wished most days, she could just press the rewind
And go back to Fairfax Farms—the good times
Times that weren't always easy—but still good

Her black-and-white stories were hazy today
Even more so, the very next day
But we'd listen with our hearts again-and-again
Just to relive them with chocolates and tea
To etch them in our memories—indefinitely

Even on the hard days, she still asks about me
If there's anything I need—if I'm happy
All sweet and grandmothery
And I know quite simply
She's a reflection of what I someday hope to be
Even though I know, it's hard getting old

The Real Me

We all walk based on some standard
That someone else created
For us to strive to achieve
And we work relentlessly to be that person
The one they expect for us to be
Even when we stray
And even when we change from their old, by-the-book way
Adapt based on what we now believe
Trying to find our own individuality
We still want to be that person
The one, they wanted us to be
Some variation of their ideal—their dream
Versus what's actually really me—my own identity
An adaptation, my originality

Somewhere there, in between the you and the me
Is the real me

Big Bad Wolf

The Big Bad Wolf knows inquisitive eyes
Dishes out his promises and lies
She trusted him deep and complete
But he didn't really care
He took it all in, and
Breathed it out like hot air

And we were all the wiser
So we thought

But they still physically fought
And again he lied, the way Big Bad Wolves do
To get through his disguise
She compromised
She left
None of us were surprised

And we were all the wiser
So we thought

Trash

Some days, I'm not feeling peppy or cute

I just simply feel confused

So I rage, in a pseudo-psychosis that's probably some mid-life

phase

Of the moon

But I'm less werewolf and much more raccoon

When I scavenge me

Tearing my art apart like trash

Finally Friggin' Free

What do you think they'd say
At the end of a hard day
When you wrecked me
And you did it intentionally

Do you think they'd all get it
Do you think they'd acquit it
I guess not—it's your high society

Or is it? I'm not sure anymore

I wonder if all houses operate this way
Passive aggressive, just to make you stay
People recklessly thrown around
And peeled, hurt up-off-the-ground

The answer, resoundingly no
And even though 'they' excused it, we still had to go
Tired of putting on this stupid spectacle—this show

It's all just a dead horse; that will race no more

We're so different; I can see it now so clear
Now, we live mostly in peace—without fear
And maybe it's not the best it could be
But at the very least, I'm finally friggin' free

I Made You

I made you
I know you don't really seem to care—not yet
But you are walking, talking, and breathing the same air as me
And I love you deep
Substantially, whole-heartedly
I would literally bleed

I made you
And no words express how proud I am
I could try here
But I wouldn't know where to begin
You are my blood, and
You are my perfect kin

You are absolutely, unabashedly perfect in my eyes
For you, I would die a million times
And come back here just to stare
Be there, and
Breathe your same air
Because, I made you

You'll always be mine
And when you're at your lowest, I'll say "it will be just fine"
I will love you until my dying day, my everyday Valentine

Divinest-of-divine
Because you are me
You are mine

I made you

Old Acoustic Mountain Heart

He found a place in the woods
To search himself for answers
To questions he'd heard before
And there, he had time to ponder
In himself, he'd ride—he'd wander
Would often get sullen, get somber
And he'd emerge with a tune
In some grand debut
That would almost knock you down
With that old acoustic sound
And a mountain heart

He'd curl his voice most days
To sound more like George Jones
And mix songs up 'bout the Bible and 'bout gettin' stoned
And we'd all laugh
Because half the crap
Weren't even the right words
And those lyrics would get more and more absurd
As we'd soak in the moonlight—sometimes all night
With that old acoustic sound
And a mountain heart

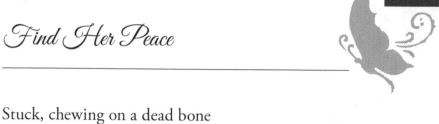

Find Her Peace

Stuck, chewing on a dead bone
Angry ole dog, sad and alone
Mad at the world
Stewing, without resolution
He waits, desperately looking to unwind
But now, she is so hard to find
Because what she seeks is simply joy
Not a fight, or another single sleepless night
She wants to find her peace
That's really all she needs

In You

I wrote about you because you changed me
In you, there was a me I hadn't met yet
And I chose you because I loved her

He Couldn't Withstand the Weight of the World

Secrets were his business
And with a little gin
Doors that were closed real tight
Would open, abruptly again.....quickly, he'd discredit them

Because he was a man
And he could withstand the weight of the world

It was so hard to contain
The emotions living inside him
He'd go recklessly in-and-out of them
Telling you what he'd seen, where he'd been

Proclaiming "He was a man!"
And "He could withstand the weight of the world!"

Maybe it was some kind of therapy
Or maybe all some elaborate lie
He would tell himself over-and-over to get by
But finally, the rage and fight fell out into a real good cry

Even though, he was a man
And could withstand the weight of the world

At the bottom of his highest-highball
He'd find his low again, then dead end
He'd surrender and laugh, saying
"It's really all good, my friend!"

Because even though he was a man
He couldn't withstand the weight of the world

A Vision

Can we be just a vision
Of the way it was supposed to be?

Reject what's real, create art that's contemporary
Be something lovely, utopian, revolutionary?

Because reality is overrated
And nothing's ever what it seems

You can only find Casablanca now
In your wildest-of-wild dreams—it's imaginary

Even though we knew, we were doomed after all
We were still destined to be an overzealous painting on some museum wall

And there, we'd never fall
Because we were only a vision after all

What Am I Doing in Casablanca

One day you'll find it
Probably unprepared
It was sitting there all along
While you were running scared

It's not a place, it's a story
Raw feelings put to words
A million of them stirring
Like a flurry of flocking birds

It will scare you, because it's open
It will scare you, because they'll see
Your heart ripped out and broken
And patched back together, haphazardly

Over time, you'll ask this question
Existentially
And that voice inside your head
Will lead you right back here to me

Deep down in that photo
Your reflection, solemn stare
Oh that brilliant artist, sitting
Waiting for me there

The End of It All

Setting it all on fire was cathartic for me
Shutting the book—end of this story
The flames of what was once so desperately me
Were maybe the new me's greatest victory

So here, I contemplated the meaning of 'End'
I walked uphill and down, again-and-again
Until it dawned on me, that I was finally free
To turn a page, optimistically and auspiciously

And so, I did
I surrendered right here, candid
For all of you to see
Resurrected the new me, through some poetry

Printed in the United States
by Baker & Taylor Publisher Services